The American Pilot

David Greig was born in Edinburgh. His plays include
Europe, *The Architect*, *The Speculator*, *Victoria*, *Outlying
Islands*, *San Diego*, *When the Bulbul Stopped Singing*
and most recently *Pyrenees* and *The American Pilot*.
His work with the theatre company Suspect Culture
includes *One Way Street*, *Airport*, *Timeless*, *Mainstream*,
Casanova, *Lament* and *8000 M*. His translation of
Caligula was presented at the Donmar Warehouse in
an award-winning production in 2003, and the Donmar
also presented *The Cosmonaut's Last Message to the
Woman He Once Loved in the Former Soviet Union*,
originally produced by Paines Plough in 1999, in April
2005. His work for children and young people includes
Danny 306 + Me Forever and *Dr Korczak's Example*,
and he has also written extensively for radio.

DAVID GREIG

The American Pilot

faber and faber

First published in 2005
by Faber and Faber Limited
3 Queen Square London WC1N 3AU

Typeset by Country Setting, Kingsdown, Kent CT14 8ES
Printed in England by Mackays of Chatham plc, Chatham, Kent

All rights reserved

© David Greig, 2005

David Greig is hereby identified as author
of this work in accordance with Section 77 of the
Copyright, Designs and Patents Act 1988

All rights whatsoever in this work are strictly reserved.
Applications for permission for any use whatsoever including
performance rights must be made in advance, prior to any such
proposed use, to Casarotto Ramsay and Associates Ltd,
National House, 60–66 Wardour Street, London W1V 4ND.
No performance may be given unless a licence has first
been obtained

*This book is sold subject to the condition that it shall not, by
way of trade or otherwise, be lent, resold, hired out or otherwise
circulated without the publisher's prior consent in any form of
binding or cover other than that in which it is published and
without a similar condition including this condition being
imposed on the subsequent purchaser*

A CIP record for this book
is available from the British Library

ISBN 0-571-22903-4

2 4 6 8 10 9 7 5 3 1

The American Pilot was first performed by the Royal Shakespeare Company at The Other Place, Stratford-upon-Avon, on 27 April 2005. The cast was as follows:

The Pilot David Rogers
The Farmer Tom Hodgkins
The Trader Jonathan Slinger
Sarah Bridgitta Roy
Evie Sinead Keenan
The Captain David Rintoul
The Translator Paul Chahidi
Soldiers Peter Bankolé, Stewart W. Fraser, Geoffrey Lumb, Chris McGill

Director Ramin Gray
Designer Lizzie Clachan
Lighting Phil Ash
Sound Tim Oliver
Fights Terry King
Costume Supervisor Christopher Cahill
Production Manager Mark Graham
Producer Denise Wood

Characters

The American Pilot

The Farmer

The Trader

Sarah
the Farmer's wife

Evie
the Farmer's daughter

The Captain

The Translator

American Soldiers

Setting

A small farm high up in a rural valley,
in a country that has been mired in civil war
and conflict for many years

For Linda MacLean

THE AMERICAN PILOT

'Politics softens everything'

Douglas Dunn
I Am a Cameraman

Act One

ONE

Farmer The American pilot was the most beautiful
human being I had ever seen. His skin was the colour of
sand flecked through with gold. He was tall and he was
strong and his eyes were as blue as the sky he fell from.
Every time I looked at him a cloud of unbidden thoughts
would rise in my mind like insects from disturbed grass.
He might have been in the same room as us but he wasn't
like us. He seemed of a different kind entirely. All the
time he was with us, I kept sensing I was only a moment
away from a moment when I would suddenly kiss him.

. . .

The American pilot was unsettling.

As far as I was concerned, the sooner he was gone
from my shed, the better.

TWO

A rough agricultural shed, built to house animals.
It is dark.

*The American Pilot is sitting in a corner. He is injured
and in pain. His leg is clearly badly damaged and his
flying suit is torn and bloody. He is listening to music on
some earphones. He sings along. His voice is weak and
tired. The song is 'Gin and Juice' by Snoop Doggy Dogg.*

The door is noisily opened.
Bright morning sunlight pours into the shed.

*The Farmer and the Trader enter. The Trader is carrying
an old rifle.*

3

The Pilot stops singing.

They look at him. The Trader goes over to the Pilot and looks at his uniform. He examines it carefully. He finds a Stars and Stripes badge on the uniform.

He smashes the Pilot in the face with his rifle butt.

He stands back.

Farmer For God's sake.

Trader What?

Farmer Steady on.

Trader What?

Farmer Nothing.

. . .

I just didn't expect you to hit him.

Trader He's American. On his uniform – that's the American flag.

Farmer Fine.

Trader He needs softening up.

Farmer Right. Whatever you say.

Trader I'm a village councillor. When the Captain comes he's going to ask me if the prisoner's ready to talk. What am I supposed to say to that?

Farmer Well, now you'll be able to that you've softened him up.

Trader Anyway, it's as well for him to be afraid. We don't want him trying to escape.

Farmer What do you mean, 'escape'?

Trader He could run away.

4

Farmer Away where?

Trader Into the mountains.

Farmer His leg's broken.

Trader He's American. You never know what to expect.

Farmer So, why not hit him again?

Trader Once is enough. I've made my point.

Farmer I've known you a long time, my friend. You're a trader. You've seen a bit of the world. I'm just a farmer. I respect your experience.

Trader I know how these things go.

Farmer But I've never seen you hit a man who couldn't hit back.

They both look at the Pilot for some moments.
The Trader is a little ashamed.
He goes over to the Pilot and examines his face.

Trader Where did you find him?

Farmer Out by. About half a mile.

Trader Last night?

Farmer Just at dusk. I was taking the sheep back over the river. I saw a man standing by the frog stone. It was dark but I could see by his shape he was a stranger. So I shouted: 'Ho!'

'Ho!'

He just stood, leaning on the stone. He didn't say anything. So I went up to him. I held up my stick in case it was someone I needed to give a thump to.

Anyhow, he didn't move and as I got closer I could see that he was some kind of a soldier.

Trader He's a pilot. That's a pilot's uniform.

Farmer Pilot.

I could see he was hurt. His face was blue. His body was cold. He looked in a bad way. He looked to me like he'd been out on the hill for a couple of days. I don't know what he's eaten. It's been cold this week and his leg's broken. When he tried to walk it dragged behind him. I was surprised he wasn't screaming, to tell you the truth. So I put him on my back and carried him here. Sarah came in last night and had a look at his leg. As soon as the sun was up this morning I sent one of the boys to fetch you.

Trader Who else knows he's here?

Farmer Well, with the kids knowing, I suppose pretty much everybody by now. I didn't really put my mind to keeping it a secret.

Trader Hmm.

Farmer What do you mean – 'Hmm'?

Trader This sort of thing is very complicated. There are all kinds of things . . . all manner of potential complications.

This is a serious situation for us. That's all I'm saying.

Something of a pause.

Farmer I'm beginning to wonder if you should have hit him.

Trader I didn't hit him very hard.

Farmer You hit him quite hard.

Trader It was a forceful push as much as it was anything.

Farmer There's a bruise.

Trader He's been wandering in the hills for God knows how many days. He's covered in bruises.

Farmer He's in pain. He needs a doctor.

Trader I don't think we should move him.

Farmer Why not?

Trader Security.

Farmer Your house is more secure than mine.

Trader You found him.

Farmer What does that mean?

Trader Nothing. I just mean . . . this is as good a place as any.

Farmer The man's wounded. I don't think he ought to be kept in a shed.

Trader We should wait and see what the Captain wants.

Farmer Look. You're on the village council. Something like this is the council's responsibility.

Trader All right. I'm a councillor, and I'm saying he should stay here. At least until the Captain arrives.

Farmer For goodness' sake.

Trader We don't know what the Captain wants.

Farmer What am I supposed to do with him in the meantime?

Trader Just make sure he's all right.

Farmer How? By giving him dunts on the jaw?

Trader I did not give him a dunt on the jaw. I was moving his face so I could see what his badge said.

Farmer Does he need more softening up, for example? Should I give him a kick? I'm sorry to be pedantic, but I don't want to get in trouble with the Captain. I'd like some clear instructions.

Trader Use your common sense, for crying out loud.

Farmer Common sense tells me he needs a doctor.

Trader Just make sure he doesn't die.

Something of a pause.

Farmer I have fed him.

Trader Good.

Farmer And he'll want some breakfast.

Trader Good thinking.

Farmer It hasn't been the best year for me, you know.

Trader No.

Farmer Just so as the council are aware.

Something of a pause.
The Trader goes over to the Pilot again.
The Pilot flinches.

Trader DON'T RUN AWAY. YOU. DON'T RUN AWAY.
. . .
IF YOU RUN AWAY I WILL KILL YOU.
UNDERSTAND?

Farmer I think he only speaks English.

The Trader mimes a man running away. The man gets killed.

Trader UNDERSTAND?

They both look at the Pilot.

I don't know, my friend. I don't have much experience of dealing with a thing like this. I'm not happy about it. A lot depends on us marking a path through this because we don't know. It could be very good for us or it could be very bad. We just don't know.

Farmer No.

The Trader gives the Farmer a few crumpled and filthy banknotes.

Trader This will pay for his keep.

Farmer Thank you, my friend.

Trader God bless you.

Farmer Go well.

Trader Go well.

The Trader leaves.

The Farmer remains. He stands looking at the Pilot.

Pilot I'm thirsty. Mister. Water. Water.

The Farmer doesn't understand.

Farmer It's no use talking to me, Pilot, I have no idea what you're saying.

He takes out a cigarette. He lights it. He smokes.

You want some? (*He offers it to the Pilot.*)

Pilot I don't smoke.

The Farmer continues to offer.

Shit. Why not?

The Pilot takes the cigarette, takes a draw and then coughs.
The coughing hurts the Pilot's other wounds.

Goddam! (*He hands back the cigarette.*)

The Farmer takes another draw.
He offers it to the Pilot again – as a joke.
The Pilot looks at him – realises it's a joke.
They both laugh.
The laughing hurts the Pilot.

Shit.

> *They both laugh again.*
> *They stop laughing.*

Water.

> *The Pilot mimes drinking.*

Farmer Water.

THREE

Sarah The story of everything, my life from its beginning
to its end, the lives of my three sons, the life of my
daughter, the life of my brother and the lives of my sisters,
the lives, thank God, of my father and mother and husband
– all of our stories from their beginning to their end, are
contained in God's mind. It is a mind that I have no
possibility of ever understanding. I can only know that
God's is a mind of infinite mercy and compassion and
I can be sure that my story and the story of every man
and woman in this village occupies no more space in
God's mind than a single blade of grass occupies in the
mind of a woman contemplating an endless meadow in
high summer. So all I can say about the American pilot
is that our encounter was simply a moment in the
unfolding – a light breeze that shakes the grass a little
in one part of the meadow – the passing of a thought.
His arrival neither worried me nor did it make me happy.
I simply took it that it was my duty to do what hospitality
required of me, that's all. I cleaned his wounds and I
bandaged his leg. I fed him. I brought him water.

FOUR

The Pilot is drinking some water. Sarah and the Farmer stand watching him.

Farmer He's thirsty.

Sarah He would be.

Farmer Trader gave me some money for his keep.

He gives Sarah the money.

Sarah What do you want me to do with it?

Farmer See what you can get for it. Maybe get some meat. See if you can find any painkillers.

Sarah Where will I find painkillers?

Farmer Maybe someone's got some.

The Pilot looks at Sarah. He smiles.

Pilot It's good. Good food. Thank you, ma'am.

Something of a pause.

Wait –

The Pilot reaches into a pocket of his flying suit and takes out a small wallet. In the wallet is a photograph. He holds the photograph out to Sarah.

Pilot Here. My wife. Francesca. My kid. Carl. Carl. This is the Georgia State Show. See? That's Carl with Daffy Duck. Daffy Duck?

She doesn't take the picture. He puts it on the ground in front of her.

I guess you guys don't get Daffy Duck.

Sarah picks it up.

She shows it to the Farmer.

Farmer Looks like Daffy Duck.

She looks at it.

Sarah They're so young.

She gives the picture back to the Pilot.

Sarah I don't like him being here.

Farmer I know, love.

Sarah I'll see if I can get a chicken from someone.

Farmer That's a good idea.

Sarah I don't think it's worth buying meat.
We don't know how long he's staying.

FIVE

Evie I had a dream once where the sky was torn open
and there was a different world behind it. I had a dream
once where I was walking behind our donkey through the
village just following where he led, and the village didn't
ever seem to stop, it just went on and on for house after
house after house for ever until I woke up, so I'm quite
used to thinking strange things, stranger things than most
people think. That's why it was no surprise to me to find
out that I had been marked out by God for an astonishing
purpose. I've known ever since I was little that I was
special and I always knew that some day my specialness
would be revealed, probably in the nature of me being
a saint, a martyr, a film star, an acrobat or possibly a
teacher. I didn't expect what happened, though – that
took me by surprise, I have to admit. Because of my
specialness I have always taken a note of things I find
myself thinking – what I find myself liking and what

I find myself not liking – because it might be important. One day I might be called upon to teach these things, or sing about them or outline them for the less well informed. So during the days that the American pilot was with us I decided the following: that I don't think people ought to be beaten; I don't like seeing blood; I don't like seeing blood coming from a goat. I don't like the smell of blood. I don't like the smell of my own blood, or goat's blood or anybody else's blood. I don't like just being lifted up to Heaven without so much as a 'please' or 'thank you' and I don't like wetting myself. I don't like those things. Not at all.

. . .

But I liked the American pilot.
I liked him fine.

SIX

The Pilot is asleep.

Farmer He's asleep.

Evie Poor man.

Farmer This man is American.

Evie He glows. He seems to glow.

Farmer Now, Evie, America is a country far away.

Evie I know that, Dad. Goodness me.

Farmer I suppose you do.

Evie I know acres of stuff about America.

Farmer Do you?

Evie From the television.

Farmer Where do you watch television?

13

Evie There's a television at Ruthie's house.

Farmer I didn't know that.

Evie They haven't had it for long.

Farmer What do you watch?

Evie Goodness me, Dad. You see television in the shop.

Farmer I see television. I see television in the shop. I'm just not sure I like what I see.

Evie Cars. Music. Indian girls dancing. That sort of thing.

Farmer How did Ruthie's dad get a television?

Evie I don't know.

Farmer Well, look, despite what you might have seen on television, America is an extremely powerful country with a very mighty army. They also have a president. The people there have fabulous riches, but you know they're also devils who have no respect for women and – look, they go around the world encouraging all kinds of debasements and wickednesses and – anyway – this is one of them.

Evie He glows.

Farmer He doesn't glow.

Evie Yes, he does.

Farmer It's just the way the sun happens to be shining on him.

Evie God arranged the sun that way.

Farmer All right.

Evie So he glows.

Farmer He's just –

Anyway I thought it would be educational for you to see him.

Evie Can I speak to him?

Farmer I don't think that's a good idea.

Evie I can speak English.

Farmer Can you?

Evie My name is Evie. What is your name? I can speak English.

Farmer What does that mean?

Evie It means 'My name is Evie. What's yours? I speak English.'

Farmer I'm not sure what I think about you watching television at Ruthie's house.

Evie How else am I going to understand the world?

Farmer Don't mind me. I'm just a jealous old man.
When I was your age –
You don't want to know, do you?

Evie I do.

Farmer When I was your age, I had an idea that I would be an engineer. It was a pretty stupid notion but I thought I would quite like to build a dam. Anyway. One day I was told I was to marry your mother and that would put paid to being an engineer. So I said no.

Evie I know this story.

Farmer Oh well.

Evie You thought one day you'd take a look and see what you were missing so you spent all night walking down the valley and through the forest until you got to the town where you found her house and you climbed the wall and spied on her in the courtyard and you thought she was more beautiful than any dam.

Farmer Well, the point is that I couldn't be a student and support a family. To support a family I needed some land. So I gave up the idea of being an engineer and I set about – and – so, well, I didn't become an engineer in the end. That wasn't God's idea for me. But you – well – things – things could be different for you.

. . .

Just be careful around the television.

Evie I never watch it alone.

Farmer You're a good girl, Evie. I hope we sort you out with a good man.
We've been looking, you know.

Evie You haven't found one, though.

Farmer They're all terrible. I haven't seen one I like. I'm going to hate it when you go. Sons are sons. They're fine but – I shouldn't say this – you can't talk to them.
Daughters are –
Well, I'm going to hate it when you go.

Evie He's waking up.

The Pilot stirs in his sleep.
  He opens his eyes and groans.

Pilot Owwww.
Fuck me . . .
Jesus.

Evie My name is Evie. What is your name? I speak English.

Pilot You speak English? My name is Jason Reinhardt. I am an officer of the United States Air Force. Do you understand. OK?

Evie OK.

Pilot If you arrange for me to be safely transported to the nearest telephone or radio I will personally ensure that you and your family are well rewarded by the United States government. OK?

Evie OK.

Farmer What did he say?

Evie I don't know. (*She speaks to the Pilot again.*) My name is Evie. What is your name? I speak English.

Pilot Miss. My name is Jason Reinhardt. Do you understand?

Evie This is hopeless. He doesn't understand.

Pilot Jason Reinhardt. Jason.
  Telephone.

  The Pilot mimics the sound of a telephone.

Telephone. OK?

Evie OK.
  He wants to use a telephone.

Farmer I don't think that's a good idea. Tell him it isn't possible.

Evie There's a telephone at the shop.

Farmer Just tell him it isn't possible.

Evie All right. (*She mimes a telephone. Shakes her head.*) No. OK?

Pilot (*realises this is pointless*) OK. OK.

  The sound of a jeep pulling up outside.
    A horn toots.

Farmer The Captain? Best behaviour.

Evie What does the Captain want?

Farmer Who knows?

Evie What's he going to do?

Farmer I don't know, Evie. Just tell the pilot everything will be all right. Tell him in English.

> *The Farmer leaves.*
>> *Evie goes to the Pilot.*
>> *She is solemn.*

Evie OK.

Pilot OK?

Evie (*sings/dances*)
I don't know what it is that makes me feel like this,
I don't know who you are
But you must be some kind of superstar.
'Cos you got all eyes on you no matter where you are.

> *The Pilot laughs.*

Pilot OK. OK.

Evie OK.

SEVEN

Captain This is my district. I am the authority. When I arrive in a village I give out money. When I eat with a farmer I talk to him about his crops. I learn the name of each man's eldest boy. Wherever I go I wear sunglasses – even on overcast days. I do these things because people expect it. If an American turns up in my district, the people expect me to know what to do with him. If I don't know what to do, the people become nervous. Personally, I had nothing against the American pilot. In another world we could have been friends. But he and I were not in another world. We were not, for example, walking together on the streets of Oslo looking for a bar. The American pilot had fallen from the sky into my district. He was my prisoner. I had to decide what to do.

EIGHT

The Captain, the Translator, the Farmer, the Trader and Evie.
    The Captain is carrying a Kalashnikov.
    The Captain languidly points the barrel of his gun at the Pilot.
    They all look at the Pilot.

Captain Has he been searched?

Trader I don't know. Did you search him?

Farmer No. (*to the Trader*) Did you?

Trader Of course I didn't search him. I just assumed –

Farmer You didn't tell me to search him.

Trader For goodness' sake! I shouldn't need to tell you something like that.

Captain (*to the Trader*) You search him.

Trader Yes, sir.

Captain Matthew – help him.

Translator Right. (*to the Trader*) You – you hold his arms. Lets see what he's got on him.

    The process hurts the Pilot.
    After some moments:

Evie That hurts him.

Captain Is this your daughter?

Farmer This is Evie.

Captain Good afternoon, Evie.

Evie You're hurting him.

Captain This is no place for a girl.

Farmer I know, but she speaks English.

Captain Matthew is my translator.

Farmer Evie, go and bring tea for the Captain.

Evie They're hurting him.

Farmer Do as you're told.

> *Pause.*

Evie.

> *Evie leaves.*

Trader The American has been searched, Captain.

Captain So. Let's see.
Some family photographs.
A dog tag.
A knife.
What's this?

Trader It's a computer, sir. It plays music.

Captain How does it play music?

Trader It's a computer, sir.

> *The Captain studies the machine, amazed.*

Pilot Sir. My Name is Jason Reinhardt. I am an officer of the United States Air Force. There is a reward for my safe return. On the other hand. If you harm me. The United States will hunt you down and kill you. Tell him that. Make sure he understands that.

Captain What did he say?

Translator It's complicated.

Captain What's the gist of it?

Translator He wants to go home. The Americans will hunt you and kill you. Some other things I didn't catch.

Captain What's been going on here? Why is the American here?
    Farmer – who have you been talking to?

Farmer I don't know what you mean.

Captain WHO HAVE YOU BEEN TALKING TO?

Farmer Nobody.

Captain Why has the American come here? Are you a spy for the Americans?

Farmer No, sir.

Captain An American pilot lands right in the middle of my territory. Everybody knows the government are taking money from the Americans. Everybody knows the Americans are training the government army. You want me to believe it's a coincidence?

Farmer I don't want you to believe anything. I just found him in a field out by.

Trader The government have no friends in this village, Captain.

Captain I'm not talking to you. You've handled this situation very badly, Councillor. Everybody in the district knows about the American. The government will know about the American by now. By now, even the Americans probably know about the American. I could do without this.
    Where did you find him?

Farmer A little way up the river. There's a big stone in the shape of a frog.
  He was sheltering from the wind.

  Something of a pause.

Why couldn't you just leave him to die?

Trader We knew you'd want to speak to him, Captain.

Farmer He was alive.

Captain Translate for me, Matthew. (*to the Pilot, shouting in his face*) WHAT ARE YOU DOING HERE?

Translator He says, what are you doing here?

Captain WHO'S YOUR CONTACT?

Translator He says, eh . . . eh . . .
  Where is the betrayal?

Pilot My name is Jason Reinhardt. I am an officer in –

Captain SHUT UP.

  The Captain slaps the Pilot hard.
    The Pilot reacts with pain.

Captain Shut your mouth.

Translator He says –

Captain Don't bother translating that, Matthew. I need to think. Where is the wreckage?

Trader What wreckage?

Captain The plane, for goodness' sake. He's a pilot – where's his plane? Where is it?

Trader I don't know.

Farmer He's been in the hills for days. It could be miles away. It must be up higher. If it was anywhere nearby someone would have seen it.

Captain You're right. Whoever has seen the wreckage of a plane will know there's an American. He'll have a transponder somewhere, broadcasting a position. The Americans will look for him. They'll find him eventually. Hell. Hell. Hell. What's on the computer? Let's find out what's on the computer.

The Captain tries to open up the MP3 player.

Pilot Hey, man, be careful. That's my music.

The Captain kicks the Pilot.

Captain Shut up.

The Captain puts the earphones on.
He listens.
He gives an earphone to the Translator.
They both listen.

Translator I think it's just music, sir.

Captain It's not music it's – I don't know what it is.

Translator It's hip-hop, sir.

Captain It could be code, you bespectacled vole. God God God.
    You're supposed to be educated, Matthew. Switch it off, it's intolerable. If it's a code we'll never understand it. I don't care.
    I'm tired. Go and get some rope from the jeep. Get the prisoner secure.

The Translator exits.

Trader Is there a cassette player in the jeep?

Captain Of course there is.

Trader I've got some stock in the shop. It just came over the border. It might be compatible. We could play it over the jeep's stereo.

23

Captain You have this sort of equipment?

Trader I have a contact in Dubai.

Pilot It's got my entire fucking record collection on it, man.

Trader Would you like me to to take the computer, sir? I could see if it's compatible with what I have in the shop.

Captain Yes.

Trader What do you want me to tell the village, Captain?

Captain Tell them the American has died of his wounds. Don't let anybody come up here. Send someone up to the stone. And send some men up to the high pass to see if they can see the plane.

Trader Yes, sir.

Captain It's very important that everybody does the right thing. Do you understand?

Trader Yes, sir.

Captain Good man. Now go.

The Trader exits.

He doesn't understand.

Farmer Captain. If you'll forgive me for speaking.

Captain Forgive you? For what?

Farmer I don't understand either.

Captain No.

Farmer This is my house. I would like to understand what's happening in my house. That's all.

Captain America has happened to you.

Farmer I'm afraid I still don't understand.

24

Captain Look at him, Farmer. He's weak – a half-jar of life. If it was a fire it would barely sustain a flame. But that tiny quantity of life is easily the most powerful force within a hundred miles of here. You may as well have picked up a stone and found yourself with a handful of uranium.

Farmer What are you going to do with him?

Captain Whatever I can.

The door opens.

Translator The farmer's wife has made us some food, sir.

Captain Bring it in.

Translator (*to Evie, off*) He says bring in the food.

Evie enters, struggles to hold the door open and balance her tray.

Captain Hold the door for her, Matthew, you barbarian.

Translator Sorry.

The Translator ties the Pilot to an animal tether. He also ties his hands. The Pilot has some scope for movement but not much.

Evie Cake, sir, and tea.

Captain Thank you, Evie. (*He takes a bite*) That's good cake. (*to the Farmer*) Your wife makes good cake.

Farmer Thank God.

Captain Thank God, indeed.
   I knew your wife's father. He fought beside me during the revolution.

Farmer Her father was well known.

Captain He was a good man.

Farmer He was a good man, thank God.

Captain So, Farmer. How's the farm?

Farmer Well. It's not easy.

Captain No. It never is.

Farmer The winter's been mild so far, thank God. It was cold, but none of last year's lambs have died. Not yet.

Captain Let's hope for a good summer. Have there been any attacks here?

Farmer Not this year, thank God. Only one last year.

Captain The government soldiers are at the foot of the valley. It isn't easy to keep them out but they haven't entered the valley. Not yet.

Farmer I'm too old to fight. Of course, my youngest son will join you. When he's old enough.

Captain I hope it never happens.

Farmer I'm sure you'll prevail, Captain.

Captain Tell me about your daughter.

Farmer Evie.

Captain She speaks English.

Farmer Apparently so.

Captain Do you send her to school?

Farmer As often as I can. If we have something for the teacher.

Captain Do you have a husband for her?

Farmer We're still looking.

Captain Bring her over here. I want to talk to her.

Farmer Evie. Come here.

Evie comes over.
She sits.

Captain How old are you, Evie?

Evie Sixteen.

Captain Are you obedient?

Evie To whom?

Captain She'll never find a man with a tongue on her like that.

Farmer I think it's a reasonable question.

Captain I had a daughter your age, Evie, she was called Belle. She was an exasperation to her mother. Are you an exasperation to your mother?

Evie No.

Captain Now, why don't I believe you?

Evie I don't know. I don't know what thoughts are in your head.

Farmer Evie.

The Captain laughs.

Captain Your voice is so like my daughter's. It's very strange. Isn't she like Belle, Matthew?

Translator She's very similar.

Captain Matthew was fond of Belle.

Evie I'm sorry about what happened to your family.

Captain Thank you.

Evie You'll see them again when you go to Heaven.

Captain Unfortunately, Evie, I'm not a religious man. I'm afraid I won't get to Heaven.

Evie Not if you keep hitting people, sir.

The Captain laughs.

You shouldn't laugh at Heaven.

Captain Your hand's a fist, Evie. Do you want to hit me? (*The Captain laughs, slightly.*) Is there something in your hand you don't want me to see?
What are you holding, Evie? Show me.

Evie It's for the pilot.

Captain What is it?

Farmer It's a painkiller. I asked for it to be brought to him.

Captain A painkiller? Did he seem to you to be in pain?
Let me see.
. . .
Excuse me.

The Captain gets up. He goes over to the Pilot. He plants a well-aimed boot on the American's leg. The Pilot screams in agony.

You're right. He does seems to be in pain. Matthew, give him the painkiller.

The Translator goes over to the Pilot.

Captain I decide. Is that clear?

Farmer Yes, Captain.

Captain I decide.

Translator Open your mouth.
This is aspirin.
Look.
It says so.

Aspirin.
Drink the tea.
It's only tea.
Drink it.
Open your mouth.

The Pilot opens his mouth. The Translator puts the aspirin on his tongue. Then he pours the tea gently into the Pilot's mouth.

Captain Ask him what his mission is. Tell him I'll know if he's lying. Tell him he'd better talk fast or I'll flay him alive.

Translator He wants you to explain your purpose. If you don't speak with vigour he will . . . take? Is it take? Separate! your skin from your muscles – you know – pull the skin away – what's that word, there is a word – flay? Is that a word?

Pilot My name is Jason Reinhardt –

The Captain kicks him again.
    The Pilot groans.

Evie Stop it. Stop. Stop it. Stop!

Farmer Shush, Evie, please.

Evie I will not shush.

Captain QUIET.

He points his gun at Evie.

Does nobody understand that I cannot solve this situation unless I know what the landscape is, I must know the landscape.

Something of a pause.
    He turns the gun away from Evie and towards the Pilot.
    He takes off the safety catch.

Pilot My name is Jason Reinhardt. I am an officer of the United States Air Force. If you harm me you will be hunted down and brought to justice.

Translator This is pointless. He's just saying the same things again and again.

Captain Farmer, take the girl and go. Attend to your farm. GO. GO.

Farmer Come on, Evie.

Evie Get off.

The Farmer takes Evie outside.

Captain Now, Matthew, at last. It's just him and us. Three military men together. Tell him he has nothing to fear.

Translator That's not true, is it?

Captain Tell him anyway.

Translator The Captain tells you not to be afraid.

Pilot OK, look. Tell your Captain my guys will be looking for me. My guys are out there right now. OK? Tell him to get me out of here and down into some place where I can be picked up. Tell him that. Tell him if he doesn't do that he will be regarded as an enemy combatant of the United States of America and he will be treated as such if there is any contact between our forces.

Translator The Captain is already regarded as an enemy combatant of the United States. Have some respect for the Captain. Tell him what business you have here.

Pilot Listen, man. Listen to me just one second. You can do what you want to me. I don't know anything. OK? I don't know anything about this shit hole or whatever the fuck war it is you're fighting here. I just crashed into a fucking mountain. OK. I crashed. This situation is an accident. Do the right thing here, man. You know what you gotta do. We all know what you gotta do – so do it. OK. Quit wasting time and get me to a phone. If I die here. All hell will break loose for you. Tell him. Tell him that.

The effort of this speech has exhausted the Pilot.

Translator He won't talk.

Captain Of course he won't talk.

Translator Maybe we should torture him. Make him talk.

Captain What could he possibly say?

Translator I don't know. What he's doing here. What they're up to.

Captain We wouldn't understand.

Translator We're not fools.

Captain Whatever information he has will make no sense to us. Because it doesn't refer to us. The information he has is about another world.
 He wouldn't even understand our questions. We may as well interrogate a word about the meaning of a sentence.

Translator The Americans will be looking for him. They'll find him eventually.

Captain Do you think I don't know that?

Translator I'm just saying.

Captain One day, Matthew, I'm going to be captured by my enemies. A rabble of government conscripts will beat me. I will be trussed up like a chicken, spat at, urinated upon and mutilated. I'll be taken to some field

31

of rubble and weeds. I'll be made to kneel in the dust.
I will have the briefest of moments to reconcile myself
to God and consider the pointlessness of everything I've
fought for. The last sensation I will experience will be the
taste of my own broken teeth. That is what will happen
to me one day, Matthew.

. . .

An American satellite will witness my death.

The pictures will be filed in a computer along with
pictures of empty desert and pictures of the sea.

. . .

Do you understand?

Nothing we can do will make any difference to our
fate.

Translator The Americans fund and arm the government.
The government are our oppressors. We should take this
chance to aim a blow at our enemies. The people will
expect that.

Captain What if we hand him back? Perhaps then the
Americans will fund and arm us instead.

Translator I don't think so. The Americans support the
government for the same reason I hate them. Because
they will do anything for money. Even betray their own
people. The Americans are afraid of you.

Captain Do you think so?

Translator They're afraid of you because you represent
the legitimate aspirations of your people. You can't be
bought.

Captain Maybe I can. They've never asked.

Translator You know it's pointless.

Captain All right. We'll keep him as a hostage. Make
demands.

Translator They'll never pay.

Captain We'll negotiate a price.

Translator America never negotiates. They don't make bargains.

Captain Everyone in the world makes bargains. It's rational to make bargains.

Translator It's not rational for an elephant to bargain with an ant.

Captain So what do you suggest?

Translator There are people who are offering a million dollars for the head of an American. We'd probably get more for a pilot.

Captain Those people are terrorists.

Translator We're all terrorists now.

Captain I'm a soldier.

Translator You no longer have the power to decide what you are.

Captain We could certainly do with a million dollars.

Translator With the money, we'd be able to arm ourselves better.

Captain It might buy us a year or two, a chance to build up our strength.

Translator We'd have to get a video camera.

Captain When you say the 'head', Matthew. What precisely do you mean –?

Translator I mean we contact these people. Come to an arrangement. A form of words. Then we kill him. Then these people send the video to a satellite station.

Captain I don't want to kill him. He's a prisoner. It's uncivilised. Prisoners should be ransomed.

Translator If you do this my way. Our struggle will be on the front page of every newspaper in the world.

Captain At the moment our cause is misunderstood by a handful of diplomats. Now we have the chance to be misunderstood by the entire population of the world.

Translator What do you think we should do?

Captain I think whatever we do the outcome will be the same.

Translator It's your decision.

Captain I like you, Matthew. Why do you stay with me?

Translator I trust you. I think you're a good leader. I also believe that in the circumstances you're our only hope.

Captain Of what?

Translator Of being able to determine our own destiny.

Captain Do you think that'll ever happen?

Translator Probably not.

Captain But you're still with me?

Translator I'm just trying to do the right thing.

Captain I'm tired, Matthew. I've been fighting in this valley for thirty-five years. Do you know how much I long to be in exile again. Do you know how much I want to go back to Oslo? To get myself a room in the Hilton and drink myself stupid – arrange for some girls . . .

Translator We need you here.

Captain Do you know how much I wish I was in Norway? With a Norwegian wife beside me? With

Norwegian babies playing in my Norwegian garden
listening to Norwegian jazz? Do you know how much
I wish I was Norwegian?

Translator I know.

Captain I wish I'd never come back.

Something of a pause.

I feel weak, Matthew. His presence makes me feel weak.
    Maybe I'm too weak to kill him. If you're so keen on
killing him why don't you do it?

Translator I would find it very difficult. I think I would
be sick.

Captain You've been on operations with me. You've
killed before.

Translator I'm always sick.

Captain You break my heart, Matthew.
    Go – leave me alone. Wait for me in the jeep. I need to
decide what to do.

The Translator leaves.

*The Captain picks up the Pilot's photograph. He picks
up the Pilot's knife. He opens it and exposes the blade.*

Lick my boot.

*He lifts up his boot to the Pilot's face. The Pilot turns
his face away.*

Lick it.

Pilot No.

Captain I won't hurt you. I simply want you to lick my
boot.

The Pilot's face remains turned away.

35

Please do it.

. . .

What's the worst that can happen? WHAT'S THE
WORST THAT CAN HAPPEN? All I want is that you to
taste the dust on my boot. Please do it. Please.

Pilot Fuck you, man.

The Captain lowers his boot.

Captain You would rather die, you child. You unbearable
child. Why did you come here? Why did you have to
come here?

*The Captain sits close by the Pilot. He looks at the
Pilot's photograph of his wife.*

She's very beautiful.
Tell me something. Tell me something that will make
this better for us. Help me. Tell me the right thing to do.

The Pilot spits in the Captain's face.
*The Captain cleans the spit from his face with a
handkerchief.*

Captain I'm sorry, son.

The Captain gives him his photograph back.

MATTHEW! MATTHEW!

The Translator runs in.

Matthew, tell him this:
There is power in the world.
And there is pain.
And the one must always be equal to the other.
If you cause pain.
You have power.
If you have power.
You cause pain.
In order for conflict to be avoided.

36

Power must be equally distributed between people.
Unfortunately.
In order to redistribute the power.
It is necessary to redistribute the pain.

Translator I can't translate that.

Captain Why not?

Translator It's too difficult.

Captain Then tell him the missile which killed my family
was made in America.

Translator He wants you to know, an American missile
killed his family.

Captain Go down to the town. Get a video camera.
Gather twenty of the men. Be back here by tomorrow
morning.

Translator Yes, sir.

The Translator leaves.

Captain FARMER. FARMER.

The Farmer enters.

Farmer Yes, sir?

Captain I'm leaving now. My men will guard the house
tonight.

Farmer What will happen to the American? Are you
taking him away now?

Captain Everything will be fine. The situation is under
control.

Farmer Only I was hoping –

Captain He'll be gone tomorrow.

Farmer Oh. Well. That's good. Thank God.

Captain Farmer –
  Your daughter.

Farmer I'm sorry about all that. She's – hot-headed.

Captain I like her.

Farmer You do?

Captain The translator needs a wife. He's an educated man. He needs an educated wife. Most of the women in the district are illiterate. Would you consider Evie for him?

Farmer I'd consider – but –

Captain If I die without a successor. My men will fall apart. The district will fall into chaos. I want the translator to succeed me. He's educated and he's clever but he's also weak. He's unsure of himself. A woman like Evie would give him backbone. I want the translator to be strong. He'll have to be strong to succeed me.
  I have no sons left.
  I only have him.

Farmer I would like Evie to live a peaceful life.

Captain If you give me Evie, I won't ask you to give me a son. Consider it. Take your time.

Farmer I'll consider it.

Captain In the meantime, take this money.

Farmer What for?

Captain For finding the American.

Farmer I didn't do anything. I just . . . found him.

Captain Put it towards Evie's schooling.
  Go well, Farmer.

Farmer Go well, Captain.

The Captain leaves. A jeep driving away.

Pilot Jesus. That guy is some kind of bastard, my friend. I feel sorry for you. Jesus. I feel sorry for you people. You people are so fucked.

The Farmer looks at the Pilot.

Farmer I know how you feel.

Sarah enters.
 She is carrying a blanket.
 She puts the blanket down.

Sarah It's cold tonight.

Farmer Yes.

Sarah There are soldiers all along the road. I don't like it.

Farmer They'll be gone soon.

Sarah The boys were excited about seeing a jeep. I had to tell them to stop climbing on it. They were sitting in it. Pretending to drive about. Pretending to fire the big gun.

Farmer They're just playing.

Sarah I don't like it.

Farmer The Captain gave me some money. (*He shows her the money.*)

Sarah That's a lot.

Farmer Yes. (*He gives her the money.*) It's late. You go in. I'll come in a while. I should take some feed up to the pasture before it gets dark.

Sarah looks at the Pilot.

Sarah He brings in an income, this one.

Pause.

Almost as good as having a cow.

Sarah leaves.
  The Farmer waits a moment.

Farmer Why did you come here?
  Why did you have to come here?

The Farmer exits.
  The Pilot looks up.

Pilot Where are you?

He prays.

End of Act One.

Act Two

ONE

Morning.
   The Pilot is asleep.
   The sound of Evie and the Farmer arguing outside in the courtyard.

Evie No!

Farmer Evie, wait.

Evie No.

Farmer Will you just listen for one second?

Evie No.

   Evie enters, carrying a tray of breakfast for the the Pilot. She shuts the door behind her.

   She puts the tray down near the Pilot. She watches the Pilot sleeping.

   The Farmer enters.

Farmer Will you stop just saying 'No'?

Evie No.

Farmer I'm only asking you to meet him.

Evie Quiet, you'll wake him.

Farmer (*more quietly*) The translator is an educated man. Quite reasonable-seeming, I thought.

Evie You told me I could say yes or no to any marriage suggestions.

Farmer I know.

Evie So 'No.'

Farmer But you haven't even met him properly. You're saying 'No' before you've even given him a chance.

Evie His glasses fall down his nose. He slurps his tea like an animal. He thinks he knows it all.

Farmer If I had glasses they might fall down my nose.

Evie I don't care.

Farmer I'm sure I've slurped my tea from time to time. If your mother had taken your attitude, she might never have agreed to marry me.

Evie Well, that would have been good. Because if you'd never married, I never would have been born.

Farmer Evie. He'll be here shortly. I want you to have breakfast with us. I want you to be polite. That's all. I'm not asking you, I'm telling you. Is that clear?

Evie How can you do this to me?

Farmer Do what?

Evie Sell me off.

Farmer Don't exaggerate.

Evie How much? Eh? How much am I worth? How much?

The Pilot groans. He wakes up.
The Farmer and Evie draw back from their argument, slightly sheepish.

Pilot Oh, man.
Woah.
Hey.
Good morning.

Evie Good morning, Mr Jason.

42

Pilot Is this for me?
  This is for me?

Farmer Tell him to eat.

Evie I am breakfast, Mr Jason. Eat me up.

Pilot What?

Evie Eat me up. I am breakfast. Eat me up.

Pilot OK. OK. I'll eat you up.
  I'm a big bad wolf. I'll eat you up.

  The Pilot laughs.

Evie He has a nice laugh.

Farmer He's just American. Don't be too impressed.

  Outside, the arrival of a jeep.
    A very loud tuneful blast of the horn.
    The jeep stops.

Farmer The translator is back.

  The Farmer exits.

Evie I know who sent you.
  Last night I prayed.
  You're here to save us.
  I'm here to save you.
  I know.

Pilot You're a nice kid, Evie. I like you.

Evie I know you understand me.

TWO

Translator Belle evaporated. A drop of water hits a hot pan. You forget a thought. There was a river once and now there is a dry bed. There was a wedding, there was a missile and Belle evaporated. She sang beautifully. Me, I have a bone in my throat. I loved Belle when she sang. I loved Belle. Not a particle of her body was left to me. My heart is made of leather, my stomach is a sea, my mind is a landscape of pain – I long ago became a ghost. When I saw the American pilot I found, to my surprise, that I wanted to hurt him. I felt as though hurting him might bring me some small relief. And when I stabbed him I felt relief – a sudden communion, as though in some way I was with Belle again. Not a particle of her body was left to me, not a particle, Belle evaporated – but when I stabbed the American pilot, I could see her in his eyes.

THREE

The Translator enters with the Farmer.

Pilot Holy shit, the nerd's back.

Translator Good morning, Jason Reinhardt.

Farmer He survived the night.

Translator It would seem so.

Farmer I suppose you'll want to be taking him away.

Translator He can stay here for today.

Farmer Right. I see.

Translator He needs further interrogation.

Farmer Right-ho.

Translator You can go now. I'll take over.

Farmer I wondered if you would like to have breakfast with us. With my family.

Translator Thank you, but I should be here, with him.

Farmer Surely you can you spare an hour? I'm sure he won't run away.

Translator I'd prefer to be here.

Farmer We could bring breakfast to you here?

Translator Really, there's no need.

Farmer It's no trouble. I'll just go and tell my wife to bring the food here.

Evie leaves.

Pilot Hey, mister. I got to pee.

The Translator exits.

Pilot Hey! Hey, come back, you fuck.

The Translator re-enters with a rusty old powdered-milk can, probably used to water animals. He puts the can down in front of the Pilot.

Translator Piss in this.

The Pilot struggles to his feet. The Pilot leans against the wall to brace himself. It causes him great pain to stand. The Translator doesn't help him. The Pilot pisses.
It causes him enormous pain. He tries to hide the pain, but it is impossible. The Translator doesn't react. The Pilot sees his face.

Pilot You motherfucker. You enjoy this, you motherfucker.

The Pilot is finished. Exhausted.

There's blood in it.

> *The Translator exits with the tin to dispose of it.*
> *The Pilot collapses to the floor.*
> *He is in tears.*

> *A moment of loneliness.*

> *The Farmer returns.*

Farmer Breakfast's ready.

> *He sees the Pilot. He pauses. Sees the situation.*
> *The Translator enters.*

He seems . . .

Translator He's all right now.

> *Sarah and Evie enter, carrying a tray of food and a*
> *carpet.*
> *Evie unrolls the carpet.*
> *They put the food in front of the Translator.*

Farmer This is my wife, Sarah.

Translator Good morning, Sarah.

Farmer Sarah, this is –

Translator Matthew.

Sarah Good morning, Matthew.

Farmer Of course you know Evie already. Evie?

Evie Morning.

Farmer Sit, Matthew. Eat.

Sarah Evie made this breakfast,

Farmer It's a pleasure to have a guest. We don't have guests very often. Sit.

The Translator sits. They all sit.
  The Translator eats.
  *When the Translator drinks tea he slurps like an
animal.*
  His spectacles fall down his nose.

Sarah, Evie and the Farmer watch him eat.

Translator I don't get meat very often.

Farmer Is it good?

Translator It's good.

Farmer Evie's a good cook.

Evie Mum cooked it.

Farmer She's modest.

Evie No.

Sarah So. Tell me, Matthew. What does your father do?

Translator My father's dead. God rest his soul.

Sarah God rest his soul.

  A pause.

What did he do – before he was dead – your father?

Translator He was an architect in the capital. He built
houses for wealthy families.

Farmer An architect. Did you hear that, Evie?

Translator He died when I was in America.

Evie You were in America?

Translator I got a scholarship to travel in America when
I was eighteen.
  My father was involved in politics. During the revolution
the regime had him executed.

Sarah How awful.

Farmer Evie's very interested in America. Tell us about America.

Translator I spent three months in New York. Then I took a train to San Diego. I spent three months in San Diego.

In San Diego I walked along the side of wide roads. I saw, in a shop, a wall bigger than your house, stocked only with different types of orange juice. One man took me to his house. He had a television in every room. Every person has a car. In the cars they play music. I didn't know anybody. The man who took me into his house tried to molest me. I was very lonely in San Diego. I spent all my money on drink and cigarettes and pornography.

Sarah God forgive you.

Translator God forgive me.

An American train is more like a palace than a train.

New York is a very dangerous place. Personally I was never robbed, but people told me that I should expect to be robbed. In New York I addressed a political meeting. A lot of people came.

They wanted to send money to help our people, but I didn't know who to send it to. I spent it on pornography. I loved America. America is the most perfect society on earth. You can't deny it. How do you explain it? Almost every day there was a moment when I sat on a bench and wept. Maybe I would have been happier in Moscow. I was a communist then.

Sarah God forgive you.

Translator I'm sorry. I shouldn't talk like this. I've been uncivil. You make a good breakfast, Evie, thank God.

Farmer Thank God.

A pause.

Sarah Tell me, Matthew. Is your mother alive?

Translator My mother lives with my brother in the capital. I have no contact with her. God willing, I'll see her again before she dies. But it's difficult.

Sarah I'm sure she prays for you every day.

Translator The Captain's men will be arriving soon. If it's possible, I want to buy a goat from you to feed them. Can you show me your animals?

Farmer Of course. I'll take you to the pasture.

Translator Thank you for breakfast.
  Nice to meet you, Evie.

  The Translator and the Farmer leave.
    Sarah starts to collect together all the things that need to be taken back to the kitchen.

Sarah Well?

Evie Never.

Sarah I know what you mean. Perhaps he's learned too much. His movements are too gentle. His eyes are too thoughtful. He doesn't look like he can turn his hand to much that's any use.

Evie Never ever.

Sarah He has a big appetite though. That's good. It's hard to love a man with a small appetite.

Evie No.

Sarah The Captain recommends him. A man changes when he gets married. Your father ate like a bird when we first met. He's more solid now.

Evie I don't want him.

Sarah He's sad. You tend to be happy. Both of you need a dose of the other. If he becomes an important man, so much the better for everyone.

Evie Never in a million years.

Sarah He will save me a son, Evie.

Sarah leaves.
Evie remains.
A moment.

Pilot OK?

Evie OK.

Pilot OK.

Evie When I'm with you, everything is clear.

Pilot Evie. Tell your father. America wants to help you. America wants your freedom. Tell your father. If they kill me – bombs come here. If they don't kill me – money comes. You understand? (*He points up.*) My guys are looking for me. My guys will find me. You gotta do the right thing, Evie. You gotta do the right thing.

Evie How can you be here? You're from America.

Pilot OK.

He reaches out his hand towards her.
She lets him touch her.

Evie How can you be here now?

Pilot Hey. Hey. Don't cry. It'll be all right. Just tell your dad – get me a telephone. It's gonna be all right, kid. Get me a telephone.

She moves back, away from him.

Evie I can't. I can't do it. I can't.

Evie leaves.

FOUR

Trader For me the American pilot just meant more work.
The Captain was throwing money around the village,
which caused arguments which I had to sort out. As usual.
There was all sorts of business about finding food and
lodging for his men. Who arranged all that? Me. These
are my burdens. All the time I walk a thin line. All the
time I'm treading on petals. I don't court popularity. I
have a stomach ulcer that won't go away, but I hide the
pain. I'm always thinking three steps ahead. Where's the
margin? Every situation contains a margin, if you know
where to look. I can find the penny under the snow. There
is a pilot. He is an American. These are the circumstances.
Where is the margin? It's my job to find the margin.

FIVE

Early evening.
    The noise of music playing from the jeep.
    The music is from the Pilot's tape. The song is 'Burn,
Motherfucker, Burn' by Metallica.

Pilot TURN IT UP.
    BRING A GUY A BEER.
    BRING IN THE BITCHES!
    LET'S PARTY.

    The Pilot laughs.

    The Trader enters. The Farmer follows.

Trader Four thousand songs. The adapters cost five
dollars apiece from my contact in Dubai. He got them
for two dollars from his contact in America. I sold the
whole lot, player and adapter, to the Captain's men for

a hundred dollars. Ha ha. Four thousand songs. That's America, Farmer. You don't have to keep anything in your head. Not even a song.

The Pilot is silent again.

Farmer I'm not sure you should be in here.

Trader It's fine.

Farmer The Captain said –

Trader Here.

The Trader reveals a bottle of whisky he has been concealing. He passes it to the Farmer.

Take some.

The Farmer takes a swig.

Farmer You've had most of this already.

Trader There's plenty more.

Farmer Do you know what's going to happen to him?

Trader Don't trouble yourself. These things are like the movements of the clouds. They take place high above us. There's sun, there's rain. That's all we need to know. Have you got a knife?

Farmer Why do you want a knife?

Trader Never mind why. Have you got one?

Farmer Yes.

Trader Can I borrow it?

Farmer I suppose.

Trader Keep watch. Tell me if anyone's coming.

Farmer He doesn't need any more softening up, for goodness' sake.

Trader Will you just guard the door?

Farmer What?

Trader Do it.

> *The Farmer goes out.*
> *The Trader goes over to the Pilot holding the knife.*
> *He grabs the Pilot's uniform.*

Pilot Get off me.

Trader Shut up.

> *The Trader slaps the Pilot.*
> *He takes out a folded piece of fax paper.*
> *Gives it to the Pilot.*
> *The Pilot opens it and reads it.*

Trader America knows you're here. I told my contact in Dubai. They want proof before I get my money. You stay here. They come here. This is your proof. Now I take my proof.

> *The Trader cuts the Pilot's name badge and number from his uniform. He puts the name badge in his pocket.*

Farmer You're all right – they're all drinking round the fire – nobody's coming in.

> . . .

What on earth are you doing?

> *The Trader gives the knife back to the Farmer.*

Trader The village was here before the American pilot and the village will be here long after the American pilot has gone. We have to look after ourselves.

Farmer They're going to kill him, aren't they?

Trader The clouds move above us, we experience the weather.
Keep the whisky. Don't tell the Captain.

53

The Trader leaves.
    The Farmer remains, holding the whisky and the knife.
    He takes another swig.
    He goes over to the Pilot.
    He cuts the rope that is binding the Pilot to the post.

Farmer Go. They're going to kill you. They'll probably kill me for this. Go.
    They won't see you. Go. Go on. They're killing a goat out there. You can get a couple of hours ahead of them – maybe a whole night – go – GO –

The Pilot doesn't move.

Farmer For God's sake!

Pilot I have to stay here.

Farmer Go.

He tries to push the Pilot. To help him to his feet.

Pilot No! No! It's OK. I'm OK.

Farmer Not OK. Not OK. They're going to kill you.

Pilot My guys are looking for me. (*He points up to the sky.*) This is where they'll look. They'll find me. Your guys are having a party. They killed a goat. They won't do anything tonight. My guys will be here very soon. Very soon. It's OK.

The Farmer looks out of the door.

Farmer It's too late.
    Too late.

He ties the Pilot up again.

Too late.

When he has finished:

Pilot It's OK. Everything's OK.

Farmer OK.

Pilot OK.

The Translator enters.
He is carrying a video camera on a tripod.

Shit.

Translator You can leave now. I'll take over.

The Farmer leaves.
The Translator sets the camera up in front of the
Pilot.

Translator You're going to die, but you don't seem afraid.
Are you afraid?
. . .
I'm always afraid. My mind is a desert of fear and
grief. All my thoughts, even gentle ones, have to survive
in that landscape. Mostly they die.

The Translator finds the knife on the floor.
The Translator looks at the knife.

The men are celebrating. Whisky and a killed goat. I don't
like to be around celebration. I don't like the singing.
I can't stand the smell of roasting meat.
. . .
You try translating these thoughts. I have to translate
your thoughts into my language. I would like you to
translate my thoughts into your language.

Pilot I don't understand. Speak to me in English. I don't
understand you.

The Translator stabs the knife into the Pilot's broken
leg.
The Pilot screams.
The Translator withdraws the knife.
The Pilot reels in pain.

The Translator goes outside the door.
  He is sick.
  He re-enters, takes his glasses off and wipes them on his shirt.

The Captain enters.

Captain Is he all right?

Translator I stabbed him in the leg.

Captain Why did you do that?

Translator I wanted to see if I could bring myself to do it.

Captain You've been sick.

Translator Yes.

Captain There's still hope for you.

  Something of a pause.

It's cold.

Translator Yes.

Captain I think it's going to snow tonight.

Translator The video camera is ready, sir. Have you written something for him to say?

Captain No.

Translator The message is important.

Captain I know.

Translator The whole world's going to hear it.

Captain I know.

Translator We can tell them what we're fighting for.

Captain Remind me what that is, Matthew. It eludes me.

Translator We're fighting for the chance to –

Captain We're fighting for small tactical advantages in a war that we'll never see the end of. It's hardly a compelling message.

Translator We still need something.

Captain We're a poor people, in a poor country, and we can muster only a very small, very poor army. In the scheme of things. We're nothing.
    If we identify ourselves, the Americans will destroy us.

Translator At least can we attach a message about –

Captain What?

Translator Justice.

    The Captain laughs.

Captain Imagine a family with a hundred servants, Matthew. They live in unimaginable luxury. One morning they wake to find the youngest son has been murdered in his bed. They know a servant did it.
    They just don't know which one. In their search for a culprit they must examine the motives of every one of the hundred servants. As they sit around their dining table investigating, they must enumerate to themselves a hundred wrongs they've done, a hundred guilts.
    Let America enumerate its guilts.
    Let it haunt them.
    Is the camera ready?

Translator Yes.

Captain Switch it on.

Pilot What are you going to do?

Translator We want you to record a message.

Pilot What sort of message?

Translator OK, I think it's on.

Pilot What sort of message?

Translator Will you shut up?

Captain Are we ready?

Translator Yes.

The Captain raises his gun. Points it at the Pilot.

Pilot Tell me what's going on.

Translator Wait. I'm just thinking. We should check it's working. Hold on.

The translator rewinds the video. He presses 'play'. He looks to see if the thing is recording.

It's just blue screen.

Captain What?

Pilot What's going on?

Translator Something's wrong, it isn't recording.

Pilot Put the gun down, OK?

Captain I can't stand this. Never mind the video.

Pilot OK? OK?

Translator There's no point killing him unless we've got the video.
I think I can fix it. I just need to look at the manual again.
Give me a minute.

Pilot Don't shoot, OK?

Captain Give me another choice, American.
I swear to God you seem to glow.
Give me something.

Pilot Please.

Captain He's pissed himself.

Pilot WHERE ARE YOU?

Translator Will you shut up?

Pilot WHERE ARE YOU?

Captain We could be in Norway.
Drinking aquavit.
Discussing our troubles.
No tears between us.
. . .
You're wet.
Yet still you diminish me.

The Captain raises his gun.

Translator What are you doing?

Captain Aiming.

Translator I honestly won't be a minute.

Evie bursts in.
She runs to the Pilot.
She throws herself down on her knees beside the Pilot.

Evie DON"T KILL HIM. YOU CAN'T KILL HIM.
If you kill him you have to kill me.

Translator Evie.

Captain Take her away, Matthew.

Evie Listen to me.
He was sent to us.
I know this.
He was sent to us for a reason.

Captain Go back to your father, child.

Evie America sent him to save us.

Translator He crashed.

Captain FARMER.

Evie America sent him.

Captain FARMER!
COME HERE!

Evie He's come to save us, Captain.
He's a messenger. Can't you see?
He was sent here to test us.

Captain That's enough now. (*He raises his gun.*)

Evie America is on our side.
He told me this.
America is watching us.
America sees us, Captain, just as surely as if we were
on television.
All the attacks.
All the awfulness.
America has seen it.
All the hunger.
All the fighting and stealing.
America has seen it.
He told me this.
We had no hope left.
We were full of dust and sorrow.
We were lost but America sent him to tell us, we don't
have to be alone any more.
We can save ourselves.
We can be found.
We can be American.

The Farmer and Sarah enter.

Farmer Oh, Evie, for God's sake.

Sarah Evie! Get up off the floor.

Captain Leave her.

Evie I know this, Captain. I know because I prayed and I can pray harder than anyone else because I practise every day. I went to the pasture just right now and I had a vision – a vision, Captain.
  I saw a vision of a new road winding up the valley, Captain, I saw a road and a car driving up the road, going fast, and I saw a dam and I saw helicopters in the valley like a flock of geese and I saw people with beautiful clothes and a bridge – and when the vision was over I heard him calling.

Captain It sounds nice, Evie.

Evie That's what America wants for us, Captain.
  But we have to believe.
  We have to do the right thing.

Translator Sir. We have work to do.

Farmer Evie, please.

Sarah I'm so sorry about this, Captain.

Farmer Come on, girl.

  The Farmer grabs her by the arm.

Evie I saw a dam, Dad, a huge dam curving at the head of the valley. A dam.

Farmer EVIE, SHUT UP.

  The Farmer slaps Evie.
    The slap is surprisingly hard.
    Evie is utterly shocked.

Farmer I'm sorry. I'm sorry, Captain.

Captain How like Belle she is.

Translator Oh no.

Captain How like Belle.

Translator You don't believe her?
  For God's sake, Captain.
  You don't believe her?

SIX

Sarah She was like her father. She dreamed things. He
was never really a farmer, he was too fond of concrete.
He dammed the river one summer out by the frog stone
and made a pool for the sheep to drink at. Eventually the
council complained that the village houses were losing
water so he had to take it down, stone by stone. He built
outbuildings. He put a new storey onto the house. Every
year he would spend a half of the feed money on mortar.
He dreamed. He drew up his plans without reference to
God. If God has given you a house with no running
water, don't make plans for a bathroom. If God has given
you a time of war, don't daydream about visiting the city.
God gave us an American pilot. God asked that my
daughter be taken away from me. God decided that
I should be left alone. This was God's plan for me. It is
painful and unnecessary to dream of a life in which it
could have been otherwise.

SEVEN

Night.
  The Captain is stripped to the waist.
  *The Captain is shaving using a milk tin of water and
a disposable razor.*
  The Translator is polishing the Captain's boots.

*During the scene the Captain oils his hair, his moustache.
He dresses in a pressed, clean uniform. He doesn't wear
sunglasses.*

Captain Pass me the glass.

The Translator passes him a small glass mirror.

Translator You know this is absurd.

Captain I want to look like a respectable officer on camera.

Translator You can't possibly believe her.

Captain I'm not some shabby provincial warlord, some unshaven hoodlum, Matthew, I am a Captain – a parade-ground commander.

Translator No one will believe her.

Captain On the contrary, Matthew – she will be a sensation.
A video message from a girl to the world. A message carried by a rescued pilot. What a story. A girl leading an army. What a story.
Like you said, Matthew. She'll be on the front page of every newspaper in the world. The Americans will be forced to support us. Are you sure the camera works now?

Translator I've tested it.

Captain She's got the fire of something inside her.

Translator She doesn't know anything about the world.

Captain She's innocent. Being in her presence – it's like feeling thirty-five years of dirt being washed off my body.

Translator What you're proposing is suicidal. You'll be killed. She'll be killed. Twenty of our best men will be killed.

Captain You're probably right, Matthew, but I feel twenty-five again. Full of heat and light. Invincible.

Translator No man will join an army led by a girl.

Captain She's a saint. A visionary. And besides, who better than a girl to lead us in this time of corruption? Who else can we believe in? Besides, when the people see me following her, they'll believe – they'll believe and they'll join us and every new recruit to Evie's army will bring two more in the next town.

Translator It's hopeless romanticism.

Captain It's a story. You're clever, Matthew, but you don't understand stories.

Translator I understand that the Americans haven't the slightest concern for us. I understand that government troops will massacre you before you reach the valley bottom.

Captain The government spies will see me walking down the valley openly – an act so patently insane that I would only do it if I knew something they didn't. They'll assume I must have air support. They'll assume I have some magical power. They'll assume all sorts of things. They'll hear a rumour that the girl is a saint. They'll be scared. They'll come to us. I'll negotiate with the government. By the time we reach the capital we'll have three thousand men marching with us.

Translator She's a child.

Captain In the first years of fighting, I dreamed of a ministry, Matthew. That was all. That I would wear a suit and I would be in charge of transport. That I would procure a loan for the building of a road. That I would employ contractors who were not corrupt. That the road would bring a small measure of development to a village in the interior. At the time I mocked myself for the smallness of my ambition. I haven't dreamed of that desk for years. My dreams have been full of a half-mile gained

64

in the valley. A trench defended. Evie is water on a dry field to me, Matthew.

Translator She's not a saint. And she's not Belle.

Captain I'm ready. I'll go and fetch her.

The Captain leaves.

Pilot What's going to happen to me?

Translator You're going to be released.

Pilot OK. You need to get me to a phone. My guys will be looking for me.

You're a military outfit. You must have a SAT phone or something.

The Translator unties the Pilot.

Translator Jason Reinhardt. Do you see me? Look with eyes. I am wearing bad clothes. I am a civilised human being. In nineteen eighty there was poetry in this country, and jasmine trees and I am training to be a teacher. I am teaching Marxism-Leninism to the children. I am in a village telling people build an irrigation system. You kill my president. You don't want any more Marxism-Leninism. I want my country. I want walk in my own shoes. You want sell me cigarettes. You want me to bring you a telephone.

. . .

You bring telephone to me.

The Captain returns with Evie.
Evie is dressed in battle fatigues.

Captain All right, Evie. Stand there.

Evie Where, here?

Captain That's it, don't look at me. Look at the camera. Is it switched on?

Translator It's on.

Evie What do I say?

Captain Just say what you said before. Just how you said it before.
About America.
Only this time, say it to the camera.

EIGHT

Trader You could call it betrayal, but I'm a trader. A trader doesn't really have enemies as such, nor do we have, exactly, friends. It's not in our nature to think that way. We have competitors, of course, and we have clients, but an enemy is someone that you refuse to deal with and a trader wouldn't last long if he refused to deal with people. The margin exists in the deal and the deal exists in the world as it is – not in a dream of the world, not in the world as you would like it to be. The margin exists in this world, not the next. So, it took time, it took me patience. But I have a telephone. I have a fax. I have contacts. I am connected to the internet. So yes – in retrospect you could call it betrayal, but my loyalty is to no country. My loyalty is to the margin. To the margin alone.

NINE

Music coming from the jeep.
'Signifyin' Motherfucker' by Schoolly D.
Laughter and shouts from outside.

Farmer Pilot. I brought you whisky. Drink it.
It'll help kill the pain.

He opens the bottle and gives it to the Pilot.
The Pilot takes a drink.

Pilot Gut rot. Jesus.

Farmer They're eating the goat. They're drunk. They're listening to your music. Apparently my daughter's a saint. I'm supposed to take you over the high pass to the border. Drink.

He passes the bottle to him again.
The Pilot drinks again.

Pilot Man, that stuff's got a kick.

Farmer You'll need to be drunk. With a broken leg, on a donkey, on the hill tracks. You'll suffer.

Pilot Man.
One minute you guys are gonna kill me.
Now it's a party and bottles of moonshine.

Farmer Put these on.

Pilot What?

Farmer Warm clothes. Put them on.

The Farmer gives him a warm coat, a blanket, a hat.
The Pilot wraps the blanket around him.
He puts the hat on.
The Farmer helps him. The process is painful.

Pilot OK.

Farmer OK.

The Farmer takes out a cigarette. He lights it. He takes a drag. He offers a drag to the Pilot. The Pilot takes a drag. Coughs. Laughs. They both laugh.

Pilot OK.

Farmer OK. (*The Farmer smokes.*)

Pilot Now I look like you. What do you think of the hat?

Farmer Good. Very good.

> *The Pilot sings along with a small section of the music.*
> *He performs the actions.*
>> *Both men laugh.*
>> *They drink.*

Farmer OK. OK.
See what you make of this.
This one's a lament.
From this valley.
See what you make of it.

> *The Farmer begins to sing.*
>> *He sings a lament.*

> *The lament is over.*
>> *A pause.*
>> *They drink.*

> *The Trader enters.*
>> *The Pilot continues to get dressed.*

Trader I brought a gun for you. The Captain said you were to have a gun for the journey.

Farmer Right. I don't know anything about guns.

Trader It's just for show. Sling it on your back. Be careful with it.
It's my gun.

Farmer I don't know how to use it.

Trader It's for show. There aren't any bullets.

Farmer What?

Trader The Captain said you should have a gun. Didn't say anything about bullets.

Farmer What's the point of me having it if I don't have bullets?

Trader The American doesn't know it's empty.

Farmer I suppose you fancy giving him another whack? Well, bad luck. The American's our friend now. I'm taking him to the border.

Trader Bandits won't know it's empty either.

Farmer All right.

Trader Don't break it.

Farmer I won't. Don't worry.

Trader This business with Evie –

Farmer Yes.

Trader It could be very useful for us, you know?

Farmer How?

Trader Evie has been blessed with visions. Visions attract people.
    If she gets on television saying that stuff – we could have the world on our doorstep. Television brings people.

Farmer Tourists – here? I don't think so.

Trader Pilgrims.

Farmer Pilgrims? Dear God.

Trader You don't have any experience of these things, Farmer.
    Perhaps I ought to manage things for you.

Farmer Manage things?

Trader It's right that the whole village should benefit from a stroke of luck like this.

Farmer Yes, well, thank you, when the first pilgrim turns up I'll let you know.

The Trader leaves.

Pilot Shh.
Shh.
Listen.

Farmer What?

Pilot Do you hear that? Do you hear? I'd know that sound anywhere.

Trader What's he saying?

Farmer It's no use talking to me, Mr Jason. I don't understand a word you're saying.

Pilot That's it. That's it.

Farmer EVIE! Come here a minute.

Something of a pause.
Evie enters.

Evie Yes, Dad?

Farmer I think he's trying to tell us something.

TEN

The sound of helicopters.
In the distance.
Getting closer.

Farmer Evie, do you hear something?

Evie I hear something.

A sound like a rush of air.

Trader What the hell is that?

Pilot GET DOWN.

A massive explosion nearby.

The Farmer's compound is under sudden and overwhelmingly massive and violent attack. Explosion follows explosion, suddenly, incredibly loudly.
    The pauses between the explosions are dark and quiet.

Evie is screaming hysterically.
    The Pilot protects her. Holds her.

IT'S GOING TO BE ALL RIGHT.
    HOLD ON TO ME. OK? OK?

Now a helicopter is hovering directly overhead.
    A hole is blown in the shed roof.
    The brightness of a searchlight above.
    A winch comes down through the roof of the shed.

Three Soldiers burst in.

Soldier 1 WHERE'S THE AMERICAN?

Pilot I'M THE AMERICAN. JASON REINHARDT US AIR FORCE.

Soldier 2 CAN YOU WALK?

Pilot MY LEG'S BROKEN.
    YOU GOTTA CARRY ME.

Soldier 2 COME ON.

Soldier 1 Go go go.

The Pilot is raised up on the winch. Taking Evie with him.

Farmer Stop. Please. Stop.

He runs towards the Soldiers.

71

Soldier 3 Fuck fuck fuck fuck fuck.

Soldier 3 sprays gunfire at the Farmer and the Trader and kills them both.

The Captain, the Translator and the Captain's men storm into the shed.

Captain Evie!

They fire at the Americans. The Americans fire back.

The last American throws down a grenade.

The Captain and the Translator are both killed in the explosion.

The bombing continues.
  The gunfire continues.

The End.